A FIELD GUIDE TO SPRAWL

DOLORES HAYDEN WITH AERIAL PHOTOGRAPHS BY JIM WARK

W. W. NORTON & COMPANY
New York • London

ALSO BY DOLORES HAYDEN

Building Suburbia: Green Fields and Urban Growth, 1820–2000

The Power of Place: Urban Landscapes as Public History

Redesigning the American Dream: Gender, Housing, and Family Life

The Grand Domestic Revolution: A History of Feminist Designs for American Homes, Neighborhoods, and Cities

Seven American Utopias: The Architecture of Communitarian Socialism, 1790–1975

American Yard (poems)

Title page: Superstition Mountain, Apache Junction, Arizona, 2001.

For information about permission to reproduce selections from this book, write to Permissions, W. W. Norton & Company, Inc., 500 Fifth Avenue, New York, NY 10110

Book design by Gilda Hannah
Manufacturing by KHL Printing

Library of Congress Cataloging-in-Publication Data

Hayden, Dolores.
A field guide to sprawl / Dolores Hayden; with aerial photographs by Jim Wark.
    p. cm.
  Includes bibliographical references and index.
  ISBN 0-393-73125-1
  1. Cities and towns–Growth. 2. Land use–Planning. I. Wark, Jim. II. Title.

HT321.H3856 2004
307.76—dc22   2004041487

ISBN 0-393-73125-1

W. W. Norton & Company, Inc., 500 Fifth Avenue, New York, N.Y. 10110
www.wwnorton.com
W. W. Norton & Company Ltd., Castle House, 75/76 Wells St., London W1T 3QT
0 9 8 7 6 5 4 3 2

CONTENTS

ACKNOWLEDGMENTS

The Graham Foundation for Advanced Studies in the Fine Arts, the Lincoln Institute of Land Policy, the Griswold Fund at Yale University, and Diana Kleiner, Deputy Provost for the Arts at Yale University, provided essential research support over several years. I am grateful to them all. In addition to my collaborator Jim Wark, among the many people who shared their knowledge of photography and planning along the way are Martha Sandweiss, Alan Trachtenberg, Jock Reynolds, Mary Konsoulis, Ann Forsyth, Katharine Solomonson, Armando Carbonell, and Alex S. MacLean, with whom I worked on an earlier project involving aerial photos. Megan Forney and Sam Ash, my undergraduate research assistants at Yale, Peter Marris, my husband and best reader, and Laura Marris, my daughter and proofreader, contributed in many ways. I would also like to thank Ellen Levine, my agent, and Nancy Green, my editor at W. W. Norton, for their enthusiasm for this project and their many insightful suggestions.

FOREWORD
by Armando Carbonell

Sprawl-watching: Welcome to the Great American Pastime

The everyday American landscape is a vast, confusing, and dangerous terra incognita, braved in recent years by a hardy band of enthusiasts in America's fastest-growing outdoor adventure hobby. These are the intrepid, if sometimes carsick, navigators of uncharted highway interchanges, the daring runners of overflowing arterials that, in full spate, become Class V rapids choked with Detroit and Yokohama iron. We have long been handicapped in our exploration of this new world stretched out before us by the lack of an aid to quick and accurate identification of its built forms, which often appear mirage-like, perceived only vaguely through a fly-specked windshield or glimpsed peripherally in a mud-caked mirror.

Help has arrived at last with the publication of *A Field Guide to Sprawl*. Thanks to its crisp aerial photographs and clear text, no longer will novices be left to sweat in anxious gridlock, unsure whether the big box looming in the power center at the next exit is a poisonous category-killer that should be given a wide berth or merely a harmless common-or-garden logo building or, if in Las Vegas, a "duck." No longer will intermediate-level "sprawlers" (a title we much prefer to the pejorative "sprawlista") find themselves in relationship-threatening arguments over easily confused species like boomburbs and zoomburbs. And what aficionado of sprawl has not felt a certain taxonomical queasiness upon entering a ruburb?

I must digress here to note a disturbing trend: in contravention of the sporting, "catch and release" ethic established over generations of responsible sprawl-watching, a small number of sprawlers have actually turned into "sprawl-busters" with the self-appointed mission of eradicating landscape "blight," spoiling things for the great majority. To such individuals I say, remember the sprawl-watcher's creed: Take only photographs, leave only fast-food containers. Sprawl, after all, is habitat! And to the sprawl aesthetes who, by taking leave of terra firma, find beautiful abstract patterns in fields of neatly parked cars gilded by the slanting rays of a late-afternoon sun, I say, yes, everything looks better at 3,000 feet, but be careful when pulling into the drive-through in your Cessna.

Equipped with this thoughtful and elegant treatment of a careless and awkward subject, the unflinching connoisseur of sprawl will leapfrog ahead of any LULUs in the path, escape the encroaching pod people, and learn to avoid pork chop lots like day-old sushi. As the late R. T. Peterson (alas, now in Field Guide Heaven) would say, "Make this Guide a personal thing." Use the index as a life list to record your progress through the labyrinth of sprawl. *A Field Guide to Sprawl* should be in the glove compartment of every single-occupant vehicle. It will be a faithful traveling companion to those bold enough to follow the tread marks of the great Dutch explorer R. Koolhaas into Junk Space. It is hoped that the author will consider preparing a companion volume to the present one, a Baedeker of sprawl, complete with maps.

Happy sprawling!

1. Decoding Everyday American Landscapes

A Field Guide to *Sprawl?*

Words such as city, suburb, and countryside no longer capture the reality of real estate development in the United States. Most Americans inhabit complex metropolitan landscapes layered with tracts, strips, malls, office parks, and highways. Widespread dissatisfaction with speculative building has provoked many critiques, but precise terms to define the physical elements of sprawl are often missing. While art historians write illustrated dictionaries of architecture and planners frame land use with legal terminology, real estate developers wield lively slang to discuss their projects. The essential vocabulary for debating common building patterns includes not only familiar words, such as subdivision, highway, and parking lot, but also the more exotic growth machine, ruburb, category-killer, privatopia, duck, and tower farm. Ordinary places that most Americans inhabit appear in this guide, illustrated by aerial photographs from across

the United States by Jim Wark. They are organized alphabetically around colloquial terms for fifty-one built conditions, from alligator to zoomburb. It is easy to look up sitcom suburb, billboard, or big box, or to browse the images, hunting for a match with local places.

Built space expresses a society's material and political priorities. Scattered across the landscape, typical American automobile-oriented residential and commercial real estate patterns are often termed "sprawl." Merriam-Webster's *Collegiate Dictionary*, tenth edition, defines "sprawl" as a verb, transitive, "to cause to spread out carelessly or awkwardly." This is a good general definition because it focuses on process. Sprawl is unregulated growth expressed as careless new use of land and other resources as well as abandonment of older built areas. While policy analysts debate the causes and consequences of sprawl, many planners and environmentalists use a working definition of sprawl as a process of large-scale real estate development resulting in low-density, scattered, discontinuous car-dependent construction, usually on the periphery of declining older suburbs and shrinking city centers.

During the second half of the twentieth century, the United States became predominantly suburban: Interstate highways dominated public construction, while automobile-oriented buildings accompanied by parking, such as tract houses, fast-food franchises, office parks, and shopping malls, dominated private building. In 2004, suburban places exceed urban ones in numbers of residents and voters, as well as new jobs. Sprawl produces landscapes at a scale more suitable for automobiles and trucks than humans, landscapes characterized by wide highways, endless commercial strips, large pods of isolated single-use development (such as malls or residential subdivisions), and little public open space.

Historian Lizabeth Cohen has traced how the United States developed as a "consumer's republic" in the post-World War II era, a society based on mass consumption of automobiles, houses, and manufactured goods, many designed for rapid obsolescence. Visible waste is a part of sprawl, seen in poorly used land, automobile junkyards, overflowing landfills, and exported garbage. Visible environmental deterioration is also an essential part of sprawl, seen in the form of decaying older neighborhoods, abandoned buildings, and derelict or declining transit systems. Although sprawl may be most obvious

to the eye at the periphery of a metropolitan region where speculative new construction is common, older downtowns also reveal sprawl because in an economy organized around new construction and rapid obsolescence, existing places are often left to fall apart.

Observing sprawl as a process is an exercise in understanding habitat. Skills in looking and listening are needed. As an urban historian who started out as an architect, I first learned to spot the signs of coming development on field trips in graduate school. A backhoe digging holes for percolation tests in a residential neighborhood suggests that someone seeks a permit for a house or a subdivision. Cows grazing near signs that say "Acreage for Sale, Zoned Commercial," followed by surveyor's stakes in the grass and the installation of high-intensity highway lighting nearby, mean a change from farmland to discount store or mall. Often the speed of local demolition and construction surprises my neighbors. Local planning offices file permits and plans, but few residents study them diligently. By the time "Going Out of Business" signs appear on family enterprises that have flourished for decades at a town green or on a local Main Street, it is usually too late for ordinary citizens to intervene.

Sprawl Talk

Well-educated Americans often lack words for the cultural upheaval caused by rapid sprawl. Naming is critical to identification. Identification is crucial to action. Specialists such as architects and planners may understand the physical implications of developers' decisions about land use, transportation, and building construction, but often they fail to explore the societal connections. Sometimes they are afraid to offend their employers. When they do speak up, architects and planners often wield highly specialized, impenetrable jargon. Architects use "archispeak" consisting of Latinate phrases like "interstitial spaces" to describe the spaces between built areas. Planners mix acronyms, legalese, and bureaucratic circumlocutions such as "non-attainment area" to describe a smoggy region that has failed to meet federal clean air guidelines. They add engineering jargon borrowed from transportation specialists, such as LOS-F (level of service, failing), to measure a traffic jam, and borrow a few environmental terms from chemists or biologists, such as hydrophytic vegetation, to describe plants growing in wetlands.

For most Americans, discussing everyday land use with architects, planners, and elected officials is difficult. Even graduate students who are training to be specialists get lost while learning how to articulate priorities for the built environment. Recently I asked advanced students in a seminar on American studies and architecture at Yale to define "sense of place" and "local character." The American studies students knew about history, literature, and popular culture, but they hoped that architecture students could provide them with more guidance about ordinary buildings. The architecture students could not do this. They suggested "sense

of place" might involve pedestrian scale, landscape, and history in New York, Paris, London, and Rome. They associated big cities with high culture and suburbs with banality. We started to discuss how to name the parts of a metropolitan region. Most of them could not define building patterns repeated everywhere, such as edge city or privatopia, despite the recent popularity of office districts next to freeway interchanges and residences in gated enclaves.

Naming is essential to defining problems, for both generalists and specialists, but bland styles of naming defy everyday experience just as obscure words do. Reference books for professionals, such as the American Planning Association's *Glossary of Zoning, Development, and Planning Terms,* edited by Mike Davidson and Fay Dolnick, or *The New Illustrated Book of Development Definitions,* by Harvey S. Moskowitz and Carl G. Lindbloom, often play it safe by defining terms for zoning legislation in a neutral way. The *Glossary's* entry for "billboard," for example, is rather respectful: "A sign that directs attention to a business, commodity, service, or entertainment conducted, sold, or offered at a location other than the premises on which the sign is located." "Sign" begs to be amplified by language conveying the aggressive size and garish designs of the billboards themselves, an acronym like JAWS (jumbo abrasive wall signs) or an environmental term like "litter on a stick."

Journalists coin many of these alternative phrases. Joel Garreau's 1991 book, *Edge City,* introduced readers to real estate jargon with an ironic summary of typical practices: "name a place for what is no longer there as a result of your actions. So one has Foxcrest Farms, for example, where no fox will ever again hunt and no plow ever make a furrow worth the name." In 1994, landscape architecture critic Grady Clay, host of a weekly public radio program, "Crossing the American Grain," published a guide called *Real Places*. Clay's entry for "hangout" engages everything from hobo jungles to fairgrounds, illustrated with two maps, one showing journeys to middle-class versus working-class bars, and the other detailing gang territories in Los Angeles. Garreau's "Foxcroft Farms" and Clay's "hangout" encourage readers to situate their everyday spatial experiences in environmental or social contexts. Development also has a political context. A brilliant phrase such as "ball pork," used by columnist Bob Herbert of the *New York Times* to characterize building subsidies for baseball teams, challenges readers to connect urban boosterism with the teams' owners and their manipulation of elected officials.

Knowing the slang phrases for everyday places sharpens observation. Because the subject is sprawl (rather than human habitation), the entries in this guide emphasize bad practices. In that sense, the definitions form an architectural and environmental "devil's dictionary," to borrow a term from Progressive-era journalist Ambrose Bierce, who targeted municipal corruption and individual greed. Bierce used ordinary words and defined them sardonically; I am using many slang terms but defining them straight. As J. E. Lighter has noted, "Slang is lexical innovation within a particular cultural context." The context is the transformation of the American landscape in the past few decades. While a devil's dictionary of sprawl may be controversial, it is intended to stimulate observation, discussion, and organizing.

What Causes Sprawl?

Often Americans say they do not understand what causes sprawl but they know sprawl when they see it. Perhaps people cannot define sprawl as a process—we react with sagging shoulders and clenched jaws. There are good reasons for uncertainty: many of the federal government's extensive subsidies for "spreading out carelessly or awkwardly" have been disguised. Four programs stand out among the many designed to encourage employment in the construction industry and promote overall growth by opening up raw land to real estate development: Federal Housing Administration (FHA) insurance for mortgages to home purchasers (1934– present); federal income tax deductions for home mortgage interest, points, and property taxes (1920–present); federal corporate tax deductions called accelerated depreciation for greenfield commercial real estate (1954–1986); and federal funding for highways (1916–present). Combined with state and local subsidies for development, these federal programs have transformed a nation of cities and small towns into a nation of sprawling metropolitan regions.

Sadly, federal supports to stimulate development have been crafted without regard for the physical damage to urban places and natural landscapes or the economic damage to large groups of people that they might cause. In the 1950s and 1960s, highway planning involved the demolition of hundreds of thousands of urban businesses and dwellings, frequently in neighborhoods inhabited by people of color. Between 1934 and the 1960s, mortgage insurance programs favored credit for men over women and whites over people of color. As a result, the American landscape was transformed both physically and economically to favor suburban, white populations and male-headed households. Income tax provisions that allow Americans to deduct the amount they pay for mortgage interest, points, and property taxes from taxable income serve to deepen this discrimination. Planner William Goldsmith estimates that mortgage subsidies cost the United States over $100 billion per year. Both mortgage subsidies and highway subsidies discriminate against renters and people without automobiles, the people with the greatest need for affordable shelter and public transportation. One must own a house to get the mortgage deductions that make owning cheaper than renting, and one must own a car to benefit from billions of dollars worth of highway construction.

There have always been poor suburbs as well as rich ones, but people in affluent suburbs receive most of the current subsidies for sprawl. For this reason, Gregory Squires of the Urban Institute has defined sprawl as "exclusionary new development on the fringe of settled areas often surrounding a deteriorating city." Even though sprawl is most visible as the affluent, new, private part of uneven development, its effects can be seen in deteriorated older neighborhoods and declining public infrastructure such as schools, parks, playgrounds, and public transit. The constrast between affluent, private new growth and abandoned public infrastructure marks sprawl as socially destructive. It intensifies the disadvantages of class, race, gender, and age by adding spatial separation. Sprawl is politically unfair as well as environmentally unsustainable and fiscally shortsighted.

Sprawl, as a process of excessive development driven by coalitions of business and political leaders who favor unlimited growth, expresses the values of nineteenth-century townsite speculators. A broad political lobby pressing for unrestricted real estate development has been powerful in the United States since the 1920s. In *Urban Fortunes: The Political Economy of Place*, social scientists Harvey Molotch and John Logan define this lobby as the national expression of many "growth machines" or "sprawl machines" operating locally. A growth machine is a political alliance of boosters that includes owners of land, developers, realtors, banking and insurance companies, construction companies, energy and utility interests, automobile and truck manufacturers, technical firms and subcontractors in engineering and design fields, and the political figures who receive campaign contributions to facilitate projects. It also involves corporations such as supermarket chains, newspapers, discount retailers, and fast-food franchises who mass-market their products in local environments. Many major American corporations thrive on the landscape of sprawl and some promote it globally as well as locally. Elected officials who object to sprawl are often compelled to work with growth machines because in the United States local governments rely heavily on real estate taxes to fund essential services such as schools.

The War on Sprawl

The Real Estate Research Corporation issued *The Costs of Sprawl* in 1974, a monumental report on the problems that unplanned, low-density residential and commercial real estate development creates for residents and for local governments. In 1998, *The Costs of Sprawl—Revisited* extended these findings. Yet the most perceptive critique of sprawl in the 1970s was Mark Gottdiener's monograph, *Planned Sprawl: Private and Public Interests in Suburbia*, an analysis of real estate development on Long Island. He explored speculation in the real estate industry, concluding that built environments which appeared visually chaotic were often the result of deliberate corporate strategy to maximize profits.

He argued that sprawl had deep roots in an advanced capitalist political economy where the production of salable or rentable space unites banking, insurance, and construction interests.

Between the 1970s and the 1990s, many groups joined the war on sprawl, including the Sierra Club, the Lincoln Institute of Land Policy, and the National Trust for Historic Preservation. They defended growth boundaries in Oregon, saved farmland in Vermont, and battled big box stores in Iowa. The Natural Resources Defense Council wrote, "Sprawling development eats up farms, meadows, and forests, turning them into strip malls and subdivisions that serve cars better than people." In the 1990s, as prosperity fueled unchecked growth on the fringes of most metropolitan regions, environmentalists mounted legislative challenges to sprawl, supported by both Democrats and Republicans at the local, state, and national levels. One hundred organizations formed a coalition, Smart Growth America.

As activists spoke confidently of "smart growth," "sprawl-busting," and "solving sprawl," their victories stimulated a conservative rejoinder, particularly after George W. Bush became president in 2000. Many trade lobbies such as the National Association of Realtors and the National Association of Home Builders joined anti-sprawl organizations in order to persuade them to adopt more pro-business views. At the same time, right-wing think tanks, including the Heritage Foundation and the Reason Public Policy Institute, weighed in with a defense of private property rights and a promotion of "free market" principles. To them, sprawl could be excused as enthusiastic suburbanization. The conservatives noted that since most Americans choose to live in suburbs, sprawl must be popular. They justified the workings of "the free market" as a vindication for sprawl, without asking how federal subsidies to developers and homeowners had altered market mechanisms for more than half a century.

Sprawl debates are intensifying. Researchers are conducting statistical studies to define sprawl in quantitative terms, analyzing population densities and distances from established urbanized areas. At the same time, architects, landscape architects, and planners are pursuing qualitative studies to establish citizens' visual preferences as part of the practice of designing better neighborhoods. Many designers emphasize residents' desire for new neighborhoods that look similar to traditional towns, including village greens, wide pedestrian sidewalks, historic styles of building, and mature trees. In *Suburban Nation: The Rise of Sprawl and the Decline of the American Dream,* Miami-based architects Andrés Duany, Elizabeth Plater-Zyberk, and Jeff Speck compare the American city to "an unmade omelet: eggs, cheese, vegetables, a pinch of salt, but each consumed in turn, raw." Arguing for "the physical creation of society," their solution is "a comprehensive mix of diverse land uses," achieved through traditional neighborhood designs. Californians Peter Calthorpe and William Fulton also support mixed use in *The*

Regional City, adding more extended consideration of metropolitan transportation and energy conservation. All of these authors advocate planning regionally, involving the public, and having governments institute good practices with their own land use policies and buildings.

Given this emphasis on positive solutions in architecture and urban design, the visual culture of sprawl has received too little sustained attention. Architects have not fully dissected the economic forces behind the built components of sprawl. Beginning with Peter Blake's *God's Own Junkyard: The Planned Deterioration of America's Landscape,* published in 1964, polemics predominate. Combating sprawl is not simply a case of countering bad design with good design, where good design creates instant community. A more sustained political and economic critique of the causes behind crude, unlivable environments is needed. The visual culture of sprawl should be read as the material representation of a political economy organized around unsustainable growth.

Reading the Landscape from an Airplane

Studying landscape history is the broadest way of looking at how a society shapes its space over time. It is particularly useful for understanding large metropolitan regions. While architectural history has emphasized the aesthetics of major buildings by well-known architects, urban history has dealt with political and economic development, and environmental history has analyzed the use of land and natural resources, cultural landscape history deals with the physical form of settlements, natural and built. This guide uses aerial photographs to represent the landscape because contemporary development patterns stretch out on a scale that ground-level photographs cannot always capture.

As a tool of landscape analysis, aerial photography has been popular since the 1920s, when Sherman Fairchild founded Fairchild Aerial Surveys, Inc., a company dedicated to helping both developers and planners. He used a fixed camera in a plane flying at a single altitude to shoot large, high-resolution negatives. These black-and-white, vertical images of the ground, shot straight down, were not easy to analyze. With vertical photographs Fairchild surveyed buildings for their owners and provided mapping services for city planners and real estate developers. He popularized the oblique aerial view as well, and built an archive with views from all over the United States.

Three decades later, environmentalists took up aerial cameras. During the post–World War II era, increasing numbers of commercial aerial photographers flew small planes, zooming in at oblique angles and varying altitudes. William Garnett called his Cessna the most expensive tripod you could buy. Commissioned by developers to shoot construction at the suburb of Lakewood, California, Garnett created a sensation. Although his developer clients wanted aerial images to provide positive evidence of their progress on a gigantic subdivi-

sion, most Americans who saw Garnett's work were stunned by seventeen thousand nearly identical houses sprouting from bulldozed plains.

Since Garnett's time, environmentalists have often used aerial photography to document difficult conditions. LightHawk is an organization of experienced aerial photographers who work as volunteers on documentary missions for environmental organizations. The Center for Land Use Interpretation (CLUI), based in California, interprets aerial images from across the country. Both of these documentary groups counter the tendency of some artists to aestheticize landscape from the air by using vertical distance to emphasize formal abstract patterns. The best documentary work stresses environmental interpretation and critique. It helps citizens to articulate their concerns about excessive development.

When people struggle to interpret their local landscapes, aerial photographs reveal the scale of existing and new development. In an era when a truck stop can be larger than a traditional town, aerial images convey the vast spread of much twenty-first-century development and can bring up-to-the-minute data on the progress of construction. Also, aerial photographs can be understood by people without technical training, in a way that zoning maps, zoning codes, satellite surveys, and traditional site plans cannot. If shot at altitudes from 1,000 to 2,000 feet, they can show building facades as well as site massing. Although they rarely include recognizable people, when aerial images are shot at oblique angles and at relatively low altitudes, showing land and buildings together, they entwine natural and constructed elements. Low-level, oblique-angle pictures can establish a complete visual inventory of a town because they can show inaccessible places such as wetlands or steep terrain, and reveal hidden sites such as dumps or gated communities.

Of course, some planning issues cannot be illustrated with aerial images. Brooks Egerton and Reese Dunklin of the *Dallas Morning News* reported a MUD (municipal utility district) scandal in Denton County, North Texas, in June 2001. Developers purchased land in an area without residents. They moved a few people into rent-free mobile homes as voters and "elected" officials to approve "huge sales of government bonds for roads, water lines, and sewer systems—which future homeowners are expected to pay for in taxes." There is no easy way to photograph a MUD scandal or the related problem of "astroturf lobbying," when major corporations use their public relations staff to manufacture so-called grassroots support. Nor can aerial photography capture the sleaze when developers hand a brown grocery bag filled with cash to a small-town mayor, in exchange for approval to build a mall.

Aerial photography used to be too expensive for citizens to access easily, but it is now becoming an important aid to landscape preservation. Recent books dealing with "visioning" and "visualization" by Randall Arendt and Anton Nelessen argue the need for professionals to convey spatial issues to the general public. Architects and planners often bring visual aids to public meetings. Photographic "visual preference" surveys are inexpensive and popular. Scale models are more realistic but cumbersome and expensive to build. Hand-drawn bird's-eye views (axonometric drawings or digital programs that simulate them) can show development alternatives, but are limited in how real they seem. When practitioners go away, often the positive images go with them.

I contend that sharpening citizens' and professionals' ability to critique bad building patterns helps them to visualize positive changes. This can be done through a set of aerial photographs in a small book or on a neighborhood website. Local aerial photographs open discussion and help to sustain it. If activist citizens are members of architectural preservation groups, they can move up in scale, from window mullions to major roads. If they belong to conservation groups or environmental organizations, they can move toward understanding the combination of natural and built environments, visualizing wildlife habitat and human construction together.

Land remains a contested economic and political resource. Major corporations such as Wal-Mart and franchise operations such as McDonald's have long used aerial photographs in combination with geographic information systems (GIS) technology to locate sites for future expansion. Developers and architects have also commissioned costly aerial pictures when seeking approvals for projects such as regional malls, office parks, and lifestyle communities. If aerial photography continues to be used by boosters to promote local growth, it must also become an essential tool for neighborhood groups and elected officials. Citizens can contrast images of a proposed development with aerial images from other towns where similar projects have occurred. Aerial images can be linked to GIS parcel maps containing data about topics ranging from vacant lands to historic structures or environmental conditions, as well as to traditional planning documents such as zoning maps and written plans. Aerials can also be paired with older maps, images, and documents for public history.

From Sprawl to Sustainable Landscapes

Thousands of communities across the United States are enacting restrictions on unsustainable growth, many of them following the advice of activist Eben Fodor, who demands that projects be *Better* Not *Bigger*. Both states and towns are updating their plans with new zoning, specific requirements for design quality, and strict limits on the size of buildings to help preserve the historic scale of older towns and suburbs. New buildings are being designed to promote pedestrian life rather than convenience for automobiles and trucks. Environmental protection for water,

wildlife, and open space is being strengthened. Campaigners against sprawl argue for a more egalitarian future, where human priorities will replace automobile-oriented real estate, and the built environment will no longer segregate people by age, race, gender, and income. Public places, scaled for women, men, and children, accessible to all, will be valued because they nurture fundamental social connections. Friends will no longer comment to friends, "I have seen your car a lot lately, but I haven't seen you." Corporations and trade associations will think twice about boasting, "What America drives, drives America."

Americans do not have to tolerate sprawl. Take this guide in hand to learn about tire dumps, mansion subsidies, dead malls, and edgeless cities. Probe the logic behind the material world of sprawl. Acres of bad building in cities as well as suburbs have blunted perceptions. Decades of accepting the ugly as inevitable have taken their toll, but American cities, small towns, and rural areas have much to offer besides examples of careless development. Learn what natural features make your neighborhood unique. Appreciate the historic buildings, pedestrian scale, and charm of older places. Challenge the economic forces behind sprawl in order to pursue a balanced, integrated built environment where social interaction and sensitivity to the natural landscape have not been sacrificed to mindless growth machines.

II. An Illustrated Vocabulary of Sprawl

Alligator

Sprawl is fueled by developers' tendency to divide lots in many more subdivisions than they ever develop. But raw land can turn into an alligator, an investment producing negative cash flow. As real estate experts Bill W. West and Richard L. Dickinson explain, "An alligator investment 'eats' equity because it lives on a diet of principal, interest, and property tax payments but does not produce income." "Up to one's ears in alligators," a nineteenth-century phrase, conveys deep trouble. While some long-term real estate speculations mature, and that could still happen in the Colorado hills in the photograph, others fade, like the grid on the desert in New Mexico.

Blue-sky, a related slang term from the early 1900s, refers to extreme speculation. A blue-sky deal is so visionary there is nothing in it except "blue sky and hot air."

Asphalt nation

The asphalt nation is the paved-over United States, according to architectural critic Jane Holtz Kay. Her book, *Asphalt Nation*, suggests that American mobility is "obstructed by a car culture in which every attempt to move is fraught with wasted motion, wasted time, wasted surroundings, wasted money." The asphalt nation sprang from a Washington, D.C. lobby in the World War II era called the Road Gang (also known as the Highwaymen) that included automobile and truck manufacturers, tire makers, gas and oil interests, highway engineers, and paving contractors. Under their guidance, the Federal Highway Administration expanded its road-building activities in the 1940s and 1950s.

Almost four million linear miles of public roads crisscross the United States, including the interstates. Ninety-four percent of those miles are surfaced with asphalt, according to the National Asphalt Pavement Association. Asphalt also covers uncounted square miles of on-grade parking, such as this lot near Orlando, Florida. An extensive paved area of the built environment forms a heat island because of the rising temperatures generated by paving and structures. Higher temperatures then generate increased demand for air conditioning, which can cause failures on the power grid. Opposition to the asphalt nation includes demands for a paving moratorium and instructions for cooling down with depaving projects from Richard Register of Berkeley, California.

Ball pork

Ball pork combines ballpark and pork barrel (a government project or appropriation with rich patronage benefits) to describe a stadium built with public funds for the use of a privately owned ball team. Columnist Bob Herbert of the *New York Times* railed against ball pork in 1998 when Mayor Giuliani proposed building a $1.06 billion stadium for the New York Yankees on the West Side of Manhattan. In the book *Field of Schemes,* investigative reporters Joanna Cagan and Neil deMause discuss many cities where taxpayers struggle with ball pork, including Denver. They note that the Denver Broncos play in Invesco Field, a new facility supported by a sales tax hike in six counties.

Opponents of ball pork believe that public funds should be used for public purposes to benefit taxpayers as a whole. They suggest that handouts to privately owned teams worsen sprawl by monopolizing funds that should be used to meet essential infrastructure needs such as public transit, child care, and schools. The Coalition Against Public Funding for Stadiums offers details on its website, www.stopballpork.org.

Big box

Big box describes a gigantic, windowless structure, usually of cheap, concrete block construction, typically sited next to an arterial or near a freeway interchange with high traffic volume. The big box, favored by retail chains, discount buyer clubs, and department stores, requires 75,000 to 250,000 square feet of space on one level and easy access by trucks and automobiles. In 2003, Wal-Mart Stores, Inc., the world's largest retailer, operated more than 3,200 big box stores in the United States and another 1,100 internationally, exporting big box shopping (and dead architecture) to Mexico, Puerto Rico, Canada, Argentina, Brazil, China, Korea, Germany, and the United Kingdom. This Wal-Mart big box in Pueblo, Colorado, is surrounded by parking designed for maximum demand at Christmas.

Located close to highways, big boxes often undercut smaller, local businesses, causing abandoned buildings on Main Streets in older town centers. A big box can also house a cineplex or a church. When designers of big boxes attempt to conceal the structure of warehouse-like discount stores behind fake facades resembling small stores on Main Streets, this is facadism. Campaigns to stop big boxes or superstore sprawl, documented by Constance Beaumont, encourage corporations to choose older buildings, such as factories or warehouses, for rehabilitation and reuse.

Boomburb

A boomburb is a rapidly growing, urban-sized place in the suburbs. Robert E. Lang and Patrick A. Simmons coined this word to describe "fast-growing suburban cities," or "places with more than 100,000 residents that are not the largest cities in their respective metropolitan areas and that have maintained double-digit rates of population growth in recent decades." They have counted fifty-three boomburbs in the United States, many of them clustered in the metro areas of Phoenix, Los Angeles, San Francisco, Denver, Miami, Las Vegas, and Dallas. With a growth rate of 5,909 percent between 1960 and 2000, Plano, Texas, is near the top of the list. A few streets in Simi Valley, California, shown in the photograph, represent a boomburb that grew a more modest 96 percent between 1970 and 2000. Occasionally a boomburb will include an edge node, but boomburbs often lack a business core.

Car glut

The United States suffers from too many automobiles. In 2001, about 280 million Americans owned 235 million motor vehicles. With 137,633,467 automobiles, 92,045,311 trucks, and 749,548 buses, Americans counted more cars than children. At the end of every vehicle's life, the automobile graveyard awaits. Some Environmental Protection Agency–authorized sites take old clunkers off the road for a price, hoping to contribute to cleaner air. Others simply stack used-up carcasses. Auto junkyards of every size and shape litter every corner of the nation, from the wide open space of Helena, Montana, to the overgrown lot in Porterville, California.

Category-killer

A category-killer dominates one part of the retail market, such as building materials, garden plants, drugs, or books. It competes with smaller stores—independent hardware stores, lumberyards, garden centers, pharmacies or bookstores—and in retail jargon, cannibalizes them. Architecturally, a category-killer usually takes the form of a big box. It may stand alone like this Home Depot in Colorado or form part of a group of big boxes called a power center.

Clustered world

Since 1950, most new American suburban neighborhoods have been constructed of similar houses sold at similar prices to families who purchase similar kinds of household goods. This Denver area cul-de-sac of single-family homes with protruding garages and backyard fences suggests residents of fairly similar incomes and shows why the geography of income stratification has led specialists in advertising and marketing to name neighborhoods in new ways. Marketer Michael J. Weiss, author of *The Clustered World*, developed a system to divide Americans into sixty-two marketing clusters that take their names from residential stereotypes. "Pools and Patios" refers to "established empty nesters." "Kids and Cul-de-Sacs" represents "upscale suburban families."

Because ethnic and racial segregation was enforced by discriminatory federal practices in mortgage insurance and highway location, and these patterns have never been completely reversed, clustered world can be a euphemism for a segregated metropolitan region with affluent white people in distant suburbs and people of color concentrated in poor, inner-city neighborhoods. For example, among Weiss's cluster names are "Hispanic Mix" ("Urban Hispanic singles and families") and "Southside City" ("African American service workers"). Advertising targeted to spatially differentiated demographic groups may use geographic information systems (GIS) to map consumption patterns. (Clustered world should not be confused with cluster zoning, permitting the grouping together of residences to preserve open space.)

Drive-through

A drive-through permits a motorist to follow arrows and drive around or into a building to purchase a product. The tent-shaped bright yellow structure in Denver, Colorado, sells fast food.

Drive-in, an older word from the 1920s, first referred to an early form of food market in Los Angeles with a number of stores sited around a courtyard for parking. The term then came to mean drive-in restaurants where waitresses served food to patrons who ate in their cars. A minister in Orange County, California, next launched a fad for drive-in churches with a temporary Sunday arrangement in a drive-in movie theater. People sat in a parked car as if it were a pew. The drive-through for banking, drugs, and fast food came later. It usually disrupts pedestrian circulation because curb cuts for automobiles interrupt sidewalks. Drive-throughs tend to be logo buildings.

Duck

A duck is a building that replicates and serves as an advertisement for the product sold within it. A tipi motel near Holbrook, Arizona offers shelter; a wheel of Swiss cheese in Maine houses a cheese store. While there are earlier precedents, Los Angeles in the 1920s boasted dozens of ducks—food stands shaped like ice cream cones, tamales, and donuts. These are also called mimetic buildings, *architecture parlante*, or programmatic architecture.

Architects Robert Venturi, Denise Scott Brown, and Steven Izenour coined the term duck in the 1960s when they drove past a duck-shaped duckling stand in Riverhead, Long Island. They contrasted a duck to a decorated shed, a warehouse-like big box building with a false front. If the false front is big enough, a decorated shed is called a billboard building. While some Americans justify ducks as zany landmarks that help people locate themselves in sprawl, ducks are always out of context and do little to unify neighborhoods. Many architects deride all overdone buildings as ducks, whether or not they sell products.

Edge nodes

Growth areas of commercial real estate have been called edge cities, edgeless cities, and edge nodes. They usually appear outside of older downtowns near interstate highways and they may also include residential and industrial areas. Journalist Joel Garreau coined the term edge city in 1991 to refer to a rapidly developing office and retail center with a minimum of 5,000,000 square feet of leasable office space and 600,000 square feet of leasable retail space, a place with more jobs than bedrooms. Garreau defined three types of edge city—greenfield, uptown (built over an older city), and pig-in-the-python (extended from a strip). Planner Robert Lang coined the term edgeless city in 2002, after he discovered that loose groupings of office buildings (or office sprawl) at many highway exits were more common than large edge cities like Schaumberg,

Illinois, or Tysons Corner, Virginia.

In 2003, I suggested that the term edge nodes covers both types and should be considered one of seven types of suburban development rather than a new kind of city, because the use of "city" is misleading to describe growth nodes dotted around a metropolitan region. These areas usually lack the public space, transit, pedestrian amenities, and overall density of a traditional downtown. Geographer Peirce Lewis calls an urban region with a number of edge nodes a galactic metropolis. Regional city, suburban city, and pepperoni-pizza city are similar terms.

The Colorado Springs "Motor City" area in the photographs opposite is an edge node taking the form of a pig-in-a-python. In the greenfield edge node around Park Meadows Mall in Denver, Colorado, at right, note the golf course adjacent to the buildings at the top.

Export garbage

Export garbage occurs when localities with an unsustainable way of life ship their waste products to other towns, states, and countries. In the photograph, barges unload local garbage onto a freighter in New York harbor. Every day, about 26 million pounds of residential and institutional refuse is collected by the New York City Department of Sanitation, and an additional 26 million pounds of New York business waste is handled by private companies. To manage this quantity, New York City created a landfill high enough to be visible from the moon at Fresh Kills on Staten Island. It is now closed. New York has been seeking new disposal sites upstate, in other states, and in foreign countries. Many smaller cities and towns export garbage, as do many affluent suburbs.

Greenfield

A project constructed on raw land, usually agricultural land, is called greenfield. A farm can be seen in the distance behind this residential development photographed in Kendall, New Jersey. The American Farmland Trust estimates that in the United States, 1.2 million acres of farmland were lost to development every year between 1992 and 1997. Greenfield development can be exceptionally profitable because raw land in agricultural areas often has fewer planning restrictions than land in town centers. Greenfield projects are a major sign of sprawl and often cause financial strain for local taxpayers who have to provide new infrastructure to serve them.

Gridlock

In 1980 two engineers, Roy Cottam and Sam Schwartz, worried about heavy traffic locking up intersections of the gridded streets in Manhattan during a transit strike. They coined the word gridlock. According to the *Oxford English Dictionary*, the term was next extended to apply to traffic jams many miles long on crowded freeways, such as this one in Vallejo, California, and then to any kind of stalled interaction or relationship. One cause of gridlock is that most drivers ride alone on American roads. Gridlock results from extended commutes when housing and workplaces are far apart, as well as from single-use zoning that forces people to drive long distances between housing, workplaces, and basic neighborhood services. Gridlock contributes to air pollution and can stimulate road rage, when frustrated motorists exchange verbal assaults, blows, or even gunshots.

In northern Virginia, where gridlocked commutes can stretch to two hours each way, informal, flexible carpooling called slugging begins at certain parking lots. Drivers called body snatchers, scrapers, and land sharks pick up slugs, strangers who ride free so that the driver can speed into an HOV-3 (high occupancy vehicle, three-passenger-minimum) lane on the interstates. The term slug derives from counterfeit subway tokens, according to Peter T. Kilborn in the *New York Times*, and the person first in line at any time is called head slug.

Ground cover

Ground cover means inexpensive, easily bulldozed buildings such as self-storage units, constructed to generate income while a developer holds land, waiting to build a more profitable project. A developer's joke, this usage plays on the landscape architects' term to describe low plants holding soil. Taxpayer is an older term for a small roadside shack, a secondhand car lot, or even a billboard used for the same purpose. Ground cover avoids an alligator. The ground cover in Pueblo, Colorado, sits next to a fenced subdivision, a subdivision under construction, and an apartment complex. Citizens looking at ground cover should ask, "What next?"

Growth machine

The federal government has championed growth since the 1920s when Herbert Hoover, as Secretary of Commerce, encouraged bankers, realtors, builders, automobile manufacturers, and road building interests to form a lobby to promote real estate development, stimulate construction, and energize the economy. Sociologist Harvey Molotch has analyzed these lobbies as growth machines or sprawl machines, political alliances of developers, business people, and elected officials. Areas designated for future construction are growth nodes or tomorrowlands, slang that comes from a Disney theme park. Opponents of unrestricted growth tally the economic and environmental costs of sprawl to advocate smart growth, slow growth, fair growth, or no growth.

Growth—the expansion of towns and cities in population, land area, and economic activity—has long been equated with prosperity. Many Americans assume all growth is good, but constant growth is not sustainable. Between 1990 and 2000 Las Vegas and its suburbs formed the fastest-growing metropolitan area in the nation, with a growth rate of 85.2 percent, balanced by increasing problems with air pollution and water shortages.

Impervious surface

Built environments interfere with natural processes. An impervious surface—asphalt, concrete, or some other paving or roofing material that keeps storm water from penetrating the ground—causes heavy runoff that erodes the soil adjacent to the surface. Runoff may include toxic gasoline and oil spills from parking areas, toxic wastes from construction sites, and chemical fertilizers from lawns. The urban intersection photographed in Denver, Colorado, shows impervious rooftops, parking lots, and streets. In suburban areas with much lower densities, shown in the photograph below, big box stores or malls surrounded by on-grade parking also create up to 450,000 square feet of impervious surface, an area the size of ten football fields. They transform the natural world around them into an asphalt nation of inexpensive parking. Design guidelines can require more permeable landscaping, including pocket parks in downtowns, planting strips between rows of cars and between sidewalks and streets, and roof gardens or rain gardens to help catch runoff.

Interstate

In 1956, after intense negotiations with the "Road Gang," over two hundred lobbyists representing petroleum and trucking interests, highway engineers, construction, and real estate, President Eisenhower signed legislation establishing a 42,500 mile "National System of Defense and Interstate Highways" to be funded through a gasoline tax and implemented by state highway departments. In *Divided Highways*, historian Tom Lewis notes highway authorities acquired the equivalent of "a land-mass the size of the state of Delaware" to site the roads. The process demolished many inner-city neighborhoods and encouraged the development of raw land in suburban and rural areas. Despite the cold-war name, the system served no defense function—the heights of the overpasses were too low for many weapons.

State highway departments built the roads and received 90 percent of their funding from the federal government, which, by 2001, had spent over $370 billion on 46,675 miles. As the largest and most expensive public works project ever undertaken in the United States, the Interstate system tied Americans' mobility to cars and trucks. The photograph of Interstates 10 and 110 in Los Angeles shows the vast scale of this highway interchange, which far exceeds the scale of any nearby buildings, except the truck city (terminal) at the lower left.

Although the Interstate system planned in the 1950s is complete, many states now engage in road-widening programs to expand both Interstates and arterials, local roads carrying heavy traffic. "Trying to cure traffic congestion by adding more capacity is like trying to cure obesity by loosening your belt," say architects Andrés Duany, Elizabeth Plater-Zyberk, and Jeff Speck. Although road-widening is supposed to ease the passage of traffic, wider streets can generate more cars or induce traffic. Complex and wide intersections also confuse drivers. In contrast, traffic-calming narrows streets, widens sidewalks, and favors pedestrian crossings. Another solution is public transit.

Landfill

Capped landfills rise like monuments to obsolescence. Overflowing landfills signal ongoing sprawl in an economy that encourages waste rather than conservation and recycling. A sanitary landfill such as this one in Trenton, New Jersey, is a site where solid waste is compacted and covered with earth, and hazardous wastes are not permitted. It is not the same as a dump, where there is no compacting and covering, but waste may be abandoned or burned. Both the landfill and the dump in Zapata, Texas, are LULUs. When towns exhaust their landfill capacity, many resort to export garbage.

Leapfrog

Like the children's game where one player crouches down and another player vaults over the first, leapfrog development skips over empty land. It may move beyond existing town boundaries to avoid local land use regulation. Leapfrog development usually lies beyond the existing infrastructure such as water lines, sewer lines, utilities, and roads, so it is expensive to service. The photograph shows an example from southwest of Denver, Colorado. When leapfrog development is both remote and dense, it may be called a ruburb. Rurban was coined by Walter Firey in 1946 for an urbanized rural area.

Federal tax policies allowing accelerated depreciation for greenfield commercial real estate development encouraged leapfrogging from 1954 to 1986. The opposite of leapfrog development is infill, new construction within developed areas. To discourage leapfrogging, Oregon has established growth boundaries, while Florida has developed requirements for concurrency, so no building permits are issued in areas without adequate infrastructure.

Litter on a stick

Environmentalists sneer at litter on a stick, a slang term for billboards. According to Scenic America's campaign against billboard blight, over half a million billboards line the major highways in the United States, although four states are billboard-free (Vermont, Maine, Alaska, and Hawaii) and more than a thousand smaller communities ban new billboards. Three major companies—Viacom/Infinity Outdoor, Inc., Clear Channel Outdoor, and Lamar Advertising Company—control most of the nation's billboard sites. The first two are part of media conglomerates operating globally.

The environmental movement of the 1950s and 1960s supported legislation to control billboards but was not successful. In the 1970s, 1980s, and 1990s, the national outdoor advertising industry expanded its activities and constructed some billboards on steel columns called monopoles, complete with neon and digital displays. They raised the size of others to JAWS (jumbo abrasive wall signs). Outdoor advertising causes visual pollution of many kinds: in addition to highway billboards such as the ones photographed in Manhattan, insistent sales pitches appear on public subways, buses, benches, bus stops, sports arenas, building facades, and the summer sky.

Logo building

A logo building is designed as a trademark that drivers can spot from a distance, such as a McDonald's with its recognizable red plastic mansard roof and bright yellow Ms formed by double arches. A McDonald's in Camden, New Jersey, sitting next to six lanes of traffic divided by a median, looks very similar to one in Pueblo, Colorado, next to eight lanes. Curb cuts for drive-throughs decrease pedestrian circulation because cars are constantly in motion—in Camden there is no sidewalk. In Pueblo, the sidewalk is interrupted so often it would not be pleasant or safe for a pedestrian. Even though curb cuts make them difficult to reach on foot, many McDonald's franchises (called McFranchises by the company) include playgrounds to attract children and their parents or grandparents to consume fast food. According to Eric Schlosser's *Fast Food Nation*, there are ten thousand fast-food playgrounds in the United States. Schlosser also documents McDonald's reshaping of agricultural landscapes through industrialized production of beef and potatoes. At the end of 2002, McDonald's operated 31,108 fast-food restaurants in 118 countries, and it continues to expand rapidly around the globe.

Logo buildings disrupt the local context in favor of advertising a product, and thus are similar to ducks. Commonly fast-food franchises, they also appear as gas stations, quick lubes, drug outlets, and branch banks. Many communities have organized guidelines to restrict logo buildings, a campaign that planner Ronald Lee Fleming discusses in his book, *Saving Face*.

Low density

Low density can be defined in terms of individuals, families, households, or housing units per acre of land. Single-family detached houses are often built at one to six units to the acre, such as these homes near Rochester, New York, in a greenfield location. At higher residential densities (multifamily apartments and mixed-use buildings with ten to forty units per acre) more people occupy less land, require fewer miles of infrastructure, and create the opportunity for public transit and pedestrian life.

Americans often prefer low residential densities, believing that generous lots keep house prices high. The largest include hobby ranches and hobby farms, with houses on ten to forty acres, and airplane subdivisions (sometimes called air parks or fly-in communities) with space for private hangars and shared runways. Because density is constantly debated, landscape architect Julie Campoli and photographer Alex S. MacLean have created an archive of photographs, "Visualizing Density," to help residents and designers visualize the effects of new construction.

LULU

A locally unwanted land use (or LULU) creates a problem for people because of the way it looks, smells, sounds, or pollutes the environment. A LULU may be an everyday project such as a parking lot. Often it is something more menacing such as a waste incinerator, a prison, or a nuclear facility, such as the one in the western United States shown in the photograph, where problems of radioactive waste have been documented. Campaigns against LULUs are also called NIMBY (not in my backyard), BANANA (build absolutely nothing anywhere near), and NOPE (not on planet earth).

Protests against LULUs in newly developing areas with affluent residents may force them to remote locations, thus causing leapfrog development, which advances sprawl. LULUs often wind up located in communities without the political clout to resist them, including poor communities and ones inhabited by people of color.

Mall glut

The United States has about forty thousand shopping centers holding 19 square feet of retail space per citizen, twice that of any other country. This excess cannot be sustained. Shopping malls developed rapidly after the introduction of tax breaks for accelerated depreciation of commercial real estate in 1954. As of January 2000, journalist Timothy Egan reported an increase in the number of dead malls (such as the Villa Italia Mall below, photographed during demolition in Denver). Malls like the one photographed in Sun City, Arizona, have room to expand, suggesting that the developer hopes to build an edge node around it, with office and industrial parks.

A super-regional mall may include over 1,400,000 square feet of retail space, multiple anchor stores, and theme-park attractions, such as the Mall of America in Bloomington, Minnesota. Down the scale is a regional mall with at least one store of over 100,000 square feet, a total of 400,000 square feet of leasable space, and a site of 30 acres or more. Smaller still, a strip mall includes a few stores along a shopping strip. An outlet mall contains only discount stores. All have tended to cause the economic decline of older Main Streets, but retail malls themselves are in trouble because of competition from outlet malls and big boxes as well as Internet shopping (e-tailing). New forms are emerging, such as the stretch mall composed of big boxes along a one- or two-mile strip.

Mansion subsidy

Currently a United States taxpayer can subtract mortgage interest and points on a principal of up to $1 million (invested in up to two residences) from taxable income every year. Property taxes are also deductible. This is nicknamed the mansion subsidy, since the size of the housing subsidy rises with the amount of the mortgage, encouraging monster houses on large lots. A tax deduction to encourage home ownership should be limited to one house at the price of a starter home.

Manufactured housing

At the opposite end of the market from the mansion, manufactured housing—the industry name for a dwelling unit or a trailer made in a factory—constitutes between 10 and 20 percent of new housing production in the United States. Once called mobile homes, now most units move only once, from factory to site, and they tend to be more popular in southern and mountain states. Purchasing a manufactured housing unit may require less established financial credit than a home mortgage, but these units tend to be small and rarely offer the most housing for the money. Although regulated by HUD since 1976, manufactured housing contributes to sprawl because landscaping for a site can be nonexistent (as seen here in Nevada), units are often crowded together, and units may become obsolete more quickly than standard dwellings. Recreational vehicles (RVs) are the mobile form of manufactured homes today.

Noise wall

When highways penetrate neighborhoods, cars, trucks, and buses generate exhaust fumes and noise night and day. A noise wall (or sound wall) is a barrier, usually concrete, erected to mitigate noise pollution. Noise walls do not work very well because on a wide highway, more noise will go over a wall than bounce back from it. Many environmentalists consider construction of sound barriers a boondoggle to benefit the concrete industry. The noise wall in this photograph from Colorado does provide a visual shield for green space.

Ozoner

An ozoner is a drive-in movie theater, as opposed to a
hard-top, an indoor theater which might have a painted
sky full of stars. Ozoners took up a lot of space when
drive-ins boomed on the strip in the 1950s, but they
have fallen to competition from televisions and cine-
plexes. They tend to be abandoned like this TOAD in
Nyack, New York, which is surrounded by big box
retail. Sometimes ozoners serve as sites for flea markets.

Pod

An area of single-use zoning (such as a shopping center or residential subdivision) located off a major road is referred to as a pod. The term may have derived from peas in a pod or from the pod people in the classic film, *Invasion of the Body Snatchers*. Long, winding roads that go nowhere characterize dead-worm subdivisions, places with multiple pods.

A pod is often a cul-de-sac, as in the photograph from Seattle, or perhaps a group of them, in the photograph from Frederick, Maryland. Pods come in all income categories. When designers attack pods as boring and inaccessible, they often advocate a livelier streetscape created by mixed uses, including housing, retail, and office space. The convoluted road layout caused by multiple single-use pods makes it difficult to go from one place to another. Pod should not be confused with PUD (planned unit development), a term for cluster zoning.

Pork chop lot

An interior lot requiring a long driveway to reach the main part of the property is nicknamed a pork chop lot. (See the longest driveway on the left in Sedalia, Colorado.) Pork chop lots signify sprawl because they indicate pressure to sell farmland. Planner Tom Daniels describes nickel and dime housing, which occurs when owners cut large lots off an existing farm, one or two at a time, often to meet rising taxes. The pork chop lots are the second row to go, after the lots with road frontage. In new construction, "too much pork-chopping" signals a bad site plan. These lots are also called flag lots, to evoke the shape of a flagpole (the driveway) and a flag (the rest of the property).

Power center

Several unconnected big box outlets combine to use the drawing power of multiple discount stores in a power center. Cheaper to build than an enclosed mall, these category-killers tend to destroy business for retail malls and older Main Streets. Vendorville is another name for a power center like the one shown in Pueblo, Colorado.

Power grid

Coal-fired and nuclear-powered plants generate electricity across the United States and Canada. The electric power grid is visible as power plants, as well as connecting wires and pylons (shown in northeast Arizona) and generating stations (shown in Hesperia, California). During August 2003, blackouts in the Eastern grid (which covers the East and Midwest) led to front-page coverage of the grid as aging infrastructure designed to serve local markets, now overstressed by excessive demand and inadequately maintained by companies concerned about profits.

Growth coalitions have advocated constant expansion of the power grid. In the post-World War II era, American corporations promoted numerous appliances including refrigerators and air conditioners requiring large amounts of electric power in order to maximize the demand for generating equipment as well as appliances. In 2003, the United States accounted for about 4.5 percent of the world's population but used over a quarter of the nonrenewable energy resources consumed worldwide in support of its dispersed settlement pattern dominated by single-family houses filled with appliances.

Privatopia

A community-of-interest development (CID) where residents are legally bound to obey the covenants, conditions, and restrictions (CC&Rs) of a homeowner association may be called a privatopia. Author Evan McKenzie coined the term to emphasize how these associations assume many of the powers of private governments, providing such basic services as police, fire, or trash collection. They may use CC&Rs to regulate paint colors, landscaping, and tenant behavior. Some are gated communities, where all persons entering must pass a security gate.

Privatopias appeal to many different income groups. According to planners Edward J. Blakely and Mary Gail Snyder, lifestyle communities focus on retirement and leisure with amenities such as golf courses. Elite communities protect social status. Security zone communities are composed of worried inner-city residents fearful of crime. The gated homes in the photograph of Littleton, Colorado, comprise an elite community, and the golf condos in Palm Desert, California, form a lifestyle community.

Putting parsley round the pig

Putting parsley round the pig means landscaping a bad spot or a bad project. Landscape architect Martha Schwartz used this phrase in a lecture to describe efforts to soften unfriendly landscapes, roads, or buildings. A golf course in Palm Desert, California, has been irrigated to create fairways and an artificial waterfall (water feature) decorated with riotous plant materials in vivid colors.

Rural slammer

Across the country, the construction of remote prisons is a growth industry involving concrete, steel, and lock-down hardware. Rural slammers connect sprawl with inner-city African American and Latino populations who have endured bad housing, failing schools, and few opportunities for employment in older neighborhoods disadvantaged by infrastructure subsidies to affluent new suburbs. Prisons are an expensive corrective for urban joblessness and poverty. It costs taxpayers more to lock up someone in a prison like Soledad in California, surrounded by farm fields, than to send someone to a university. The Justice Department reported 2,019,234 people incarcerated in the United States in 2002. The United States has one of the highest rates of imprisonment in the world, and the number of inmates is four times what it was in the mid-1970s.

Sitcom suburb

Neighborhoods of traditional Cape Cod or Colonial houses with neat front lawns, like these in Rochester, New York, first became popular in the late 1940s and 1950s, at the same time as television sitcoms (situation comedies). *Ozzie and Harriet, Leave It to Beaver,* and *Father Knows Best* featured model families with an employed father, a stay-at-home mother, and two or more children. I coined the term sitcom suburb in *Building Suburbia* to describe post–World War II suburbs financed by FHA (Federal Housing Administration) mortgages, but these were also called mass suburbs, automobile suburbs, and Levittowns. The famous Levittown of about eighty thousand people constructed in the late 1940s on Long Island lacked sewers, giving rise to the term septic-tank suburb. At that time, the FHA often permitted developers to avoid the cost of needed infrastructure.

Snout house

In this neighborhood, it is difficult to see residents' activities since protruding garages take up most of the street frontage, minimize the lawns, and eliminate easy surveillance of children's play. A street of snout houses fails the "Trick-or-Treat Test" proposed by Portland, Oregon, official Charles Hales, who wanted children (and everyone else) to be able to find the doors. Ruth Knack reports that Portland regulated protruding garages in 1999, limiting the front of the garage to half the total house frontage and requiring the door of the house to be no more than 8 feet behind the front of the garage. One design alternative is a narrow alley or a rear lane leading to a garage at the back of the house.

Starter castle

Starter castle describes a house of exaggerated size and aspirations, a play on "starter house," a house for the first-time home buyer. In 1904 in *The American Scene*, Henry James critiqued houses with "their candid look of having cost as much as they knew how. Unmistakably they all proclaimed it—they would have cost still more had the way but been shown them; and meanwhile, they added as with one voice, they would take a fresh start as soon as ever it should be." In the same era, economist Thorstein Veblen mocked "conspicuous consumption." Starter castles like this one in New York are usually custom-designed for the owners by architects.

Sometimes a starter castle is built on the site of a tear-down, an older house, usually in a desirable neighborhood, purchased for its lot value and demolished in order to build a larger structure. While tear-down used to refer to dilapidated houses, in the 1990s tear-downs included eighteenth-century saltboxes, Victorian shingle beach cottages, and modernist houses all sacrificed to starter castles. Scrapers, a developers' derogatory term for tear-downs in Portland, Oregon, so enraged residents that they mounted effective preservation campaigns.

Streetcar buildout

Between 1870 and 1910, horsecars and then electric streetcars carried people to lots subdivided by speculators who often owned the transit lines. With the creation of vast neighborhoods of one-, two-, and three-family houses for working people, many cities doubled and tripled in size. Developments of duplexes like the one in the photograph of Roebling, New Jersey, could occur inside city lines as well as in satellite industrial towns and adjacent suburbs. Many streetcar buildouts were unplanned growth, but these neighborhoods were denser than the sitcom suburbs of the 1950s because they were not designed for private automobiles.

Strip

An arterial road lined with automobile-oriented uses such as gas stations, tire stores, tourist courts, diners, ice cream stands, and hot dog stands became known as a strip in the 1920s, and was also called a hot-dog trail, ribbon development, and taxpayer strip. The term may derive from strip maps showing the line of a road and adjacent places. Historian Chester Liebs calls typical strip buildings "architecture for speed-reading." Almost every town has a strip these days, such as this modest example from Michigan. The most famous examples are the Sunset Strip in West Hollywood, California, and the strip of gambling casinos in Las Vegas, Nevada. In "Other-Directed Houses," an essay from the late 1950s, J. B. Jackson commented that a strip was best viewed at night from a plane as a string of distant neon lights.

Tank farm

Tankers transfer oil or liquid natural gas into storage at a tank farm. This familiar part of the infrastructure for energy consumption is shown in the port of Houston, Texas. According to the U.S. Department of Energy, of all the energy resources Americans consume, about 39 percent is oil; 23 percent, natural gas; 23 percent, coal; 7 percent, nuclear; and 6 percent, renewable. Current U.S. energy policy does not emphasize renewable energy sources or energy conservation. Over half of the oil consumed annually in this country is imported from foreign countries, including Iraq.

Theming

Theme—first a noun and then an adjective—has recently been used as a verb. Theming describes designing and decorating restaurants, hotels, shopping malls, casinos, and even small towns to exaggerate stereotypes and re-create lost places. On the Las Vegas strip, the Venetian hotel and casino replicates parts of Venice, Italy, with a palace and a campanile.

Theming has been popular since Disneyland opened in Anaheim, California, in 1955 as a theme park. Hyped on Walt Disney's television show as "the happiest place on earth," Disneyland's attractions included "Main Street," echoing a traditional small American town but hiding a shopping mall; "Autopia," a miniature freeway landscape; as well as "Adventureland," "Fantasyland," and "Tomorrowland."

In the nineteenth century, a themester was an unsuccessful derivative poet. Themesters now make big buildings.

Tire dump

Sprawl depends on millions of automobiles and just as the carcasses of vehicles wind up in automobile grave-yards, so worn-out tires rest on tire dumps and tire mountains. In a single recent year the United States generated 270 million scrap tires. In 2000, waste tires sitting on stockpiles nationally totaled 500 million. Pollution oozes from them and fires are common. Some states have instituted waste tire management programs through their departments of environmental quality. This photograph of stacked tires was taken in Midway, Colorado.

TOAD

Coined by planners and lawyers, TOAD is an acronym for a temporary, obsolete, abandoned, or derelict site. Journalist Grady Clay notes, "TOADs owe their on-ground existence to the use, abandonment, and reuse of real estate as exaggerated by a capitalistic system." TOADs may be abandoned shopping malls, empty big boxes, or closed industrial sites, such as this abandoned blast furnace in Youngstown, Ohio, which marks the decline of heavy industry in the Midwest. A TOAD in a brownfield sits on a site with documented or suspected environmental contamination.

Tower farm

A tower farm clusters several monopoles, such as these broadcast towers in Tonopah, Nevada. Cell towers are even more common—over 147,000 have been constructed to carry signals for cell phones as rival companies spar for customers. The federal Telecommunications Act of 1996, section 704, guaranteed companies the right to erect cell towers, overriding local zoning, although many health questions about cell phones and towers remain unresolved because human responses to electromagnetic fields are still poorly understood.

Tall towers—either monopoles or tower farms—are out of scale in residential neighborhoods. They mar views, especially when ridgelines sprout five or six unsightly structures from competing companies. Through what is called stealth siting, towers can be hidden in church steeples or farm silos, but this does nothing to minimize the possible environmental hazards to churchgoers or farm workers. Over 154 million Americans acquired cell phones between 1992 and 2004, and towers proliferate as more cell phones appear. As with billboards, land speculators seek permits to erect towers and tower farms in advance of demand, anticipating future sales and rentals to communications companies.

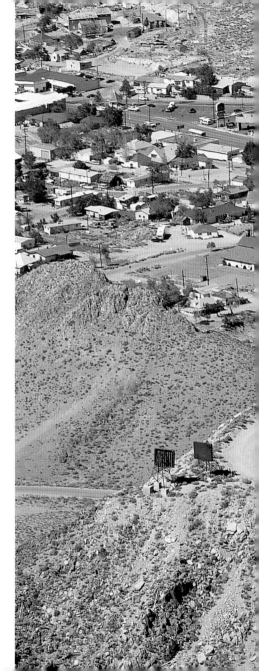

Tract mansion

A large, expensive house (usually over 4,000 square feet) constructed among homes that are very similar by a subdivider who builds on speculation is a tract mansion. Architecture critic Ada Louise Huxtable names them McMansions, where the "preferred style is Grotesquely Grandiose. Unencumbered by architects or accuracy, developers offer a mind-boggling mix of Rapunzel towers and pretend Palladian, Jacuzzis, and surround-sound." A North Dallas Special is a tract mansion with an overly elaborate roofline meant to impress a potential purchaser or visitor. The North Dallas Special recalls the obsessions of Andrew Jackson Downing, tastemaker of the nineteenth century, who added elaborate roofscapes to farmhouses he considered too plain for gentlemen. The tract mansions in the photograph are in Colorado, and yes, there are horses in the background.

A tract mansion may also be called a twenty-minute house since a realtor shows it quickly—all of the builder's energy has been focused on the front. A tract house pumped up to very substantial size through expansion is a house-on-steroids. If size is achieved by adding to a smaller house, the original structure may serve as an entry or as a first floor. New houses grow larger every decade, averaging about 800 square feet in the 1950s, and 2,200 square feet in 2000, despite shrinking household sizes. A house that includes a substantial amount of space used for work at home has been called an un-private house, flex-house, live/work house, and electronic cottage. A house with a guest house, granny house, echo house, or accessory apartment offers a second unit, usually built over the garage or in the rear yard, that may be either an office or a dwelling.

Truck city

Ranging in scale from the massive truck/rail terminal in West Memphis, Arkansas, where transfers from rail to truck take place, to the modest truck stop on I-10 in Wilcox, Arizona, facilities to serve over 92 million trucks are familiar parts of the American landscape. John Brinckerhoff Jackson's essay "Truck City" celebrates the contributions of trucks and truckers to the decentralization of American business. Since the 1950s, truckers have wielded power as a lobby. Current federal regulations cover the interstate highways and 160,000 miles of other roads in the National Network for Large Trucks. These roads allow trucks 102 inches wide. They may be single tractor-trailers 48 feet long or tractors pulling two 28-foot-long trailers. The size of these vehicles creates pressure to widen all other roads and driveways for the convenience of truckers. Making spaces to fit the trucks destroys the historic scale of the built environment in towns and cities and promotes the big box.

Valhalla

An attractive town adopted as a favorite spot by the super-rich may not be obvious as sprawl, but it will attract starter castles and experience tear-downs. Author Joel Kotkin has coined the term Valhalla for these retreats, many launched by profits in the dot.com world as part of a larger digital geography. Camden, Maine, is one of his examples.

Water feature

Any artificially constructed display of water—either active, such as a fountain or a waterfall, or passive, such as a pool or canal—is a water feature in developer slang. Water features are part of sprawl because developers frequently disregard the limits of the natural environment. Often new development removes indigenous vegetation, bulldozes topography, and changes drainage patterns. When large amounts of impervious surface are introduced in the built environment, retention basins may be required for storm water runoff, but they are advertised as amenities and usually add to the price. Two artificial marinas within a subdivision in the Mohave Desert in California almost appear to be a mirage. Narrow artificial canals divide "waterfront" houses photographed in Parker, Arizona.

Zoomburb

A place growing even faster than a boomburb, zoom-burb is a Charlottesville, Virginia, newspaper's coinage for a sprawling area. Sun City, Arizona, fits the bill.

SOURCES

A Note on Sources

A few of the words and phrases in this vocabulary appear in ordinary dictionaries, but many are fairly new and specialized in their usage. More terms show up in glossaries of urban planning or real estate. Some are found in dictionaries of American slang. Sources for each caption are listed here, followed by a selected bibliography including reference works, cited works, further reading, and useful websites. Readers' comments, critiques, refinements, and submissions of additional words are welcome. How do people talk about sprawl in your area? (Contact me at dolores.hayden@yale.edu).

Sources for Captions

Alligator: West and Dickinson; Lighter; Reilly.
Asphalt nation: Kay; Rose; Register.
Ball pork: Herbert; Cagan and deMause.
Big box: Davidson and Dolnick; Beaumont (1994); Beaumont (1997).
Boomburb: Lang and Simmons; Katz and Lang.
Car glut: Kay; Downs (1992); Rose; Blake; Goldsmith.
Category-killer: Beaumont (1994); Beaumont (1997); Peirce; Gratz and Mintz.
Clustered world: Weiss.
Drive-through: Davidson and Dolnick; Longstreth (2000); Hayden (2003); Liebs.
Duck: Venturi, Scott Brown, and Izenour; Blake.
Edge nodes: Garreau; Hayden (2003); Lang (2000); Lang (2003); Lewis, P.
Export garbage: Miller, B.; Lipton.
Greenfield: Merriam-Webster; Davidson and Dolnick.
Gridlock: Oxford English Dictionary; Chapman; Kay; Kilborn.
Ground cover: Garreau.
Growth machine: Davidson and Dolnick; Clay (1994); Molotch; Molotch and Logan; Katz and Lang; Daniels; Weitz.
Impervious surface: Moskowitz and Lindbloom; Davidson and Dolnick.
Interstate: Merriam-Webster; Moskowitz and Lindbloom; Kay; Rose; Lewis, T.
Landfill: Merriam-Webster; Moskowitz and Lindbloom; Davidson and Dolnick; Miller, B.
Leapfrog: Davidson and Dolnick; West and Dickinson; Lewis, P.; Firey.
Litter-on-a-stick: Miller, J.; Haberman; Gudis; Floyd and Shedd.
Logo building: Fleming; Schlosser; Beaumont (1997).
Low density: Moskowitz and Lindbloom; Kilborn; Campoli and MacLean.
LULU: Davidson and Dolnick; Clay (1994); Garreau.
Mall glut: Longstreth (1997); Hayden (2003); Liebs; Egan.
Mansion subsidy: Goldsmith; Feagin and Parker; Hayden (2003); Daniels.
Manufactured housing: West and Dickinson; Moskowitz and Lindbloom; Davidson and Dolnick.
Noise wall: Gellner; Moskowitz and Lindbloom.
Ozoner: Lighter; Valentine.
Pod: Chapman; Duany, Plater-Zyberk, and Speck.
Pork chop lot: Moskowitz and Lindbloom; Davidson and Dolnick; Daniels.
Power center: Beaumont (1994); Beaumont (1997); Peirce.
Power grid: Banerjee and Firestone.

Privatopia: McKenzie; Blakely and Snyder.

Put parsley round the pig: used in lecture by Martha Schwartz.

Rural slammer: Chapman; Butterfield; Abramsky.

Sitcom suburb: Hayden (2003); Marling; Rome.

Snout house: Knack; Noll and Scupelli.

Starter castle: West and Dickinson; Huxtable; Hayden (2002).

Streetcar buildout: Hayden (2003).

Strip: Oxford English Dictionary; Chapman; Davidson and Dolnick; Moskowitz and Lindbloom; West and Dickinson; Liebs; Longstreth (2000); Jackson (1997); Clay (1980).

Tank farm: Oxford English Dictionary; Moskowitz and Lindbloom; Davidson and Dolnick.

Theming: Huxtable; Marling.

Tire dump: Clay (1994); Kay.

TOAD: Clay (1994); Greenberg, Popper, and West.

Tower farm: Levitt; Selingo; Woodside; Wikle.

Tract mansion: Huxtable; Duany, Plater-Zyberk, and Speck; Garreau.

Truck city: Jackson (1992); Davidson and Dolnick.

Water feature: Garreau; Rome.

Valhalla: Kotkin; Kotkin and Siegel.

Zoomburb: *Charlottesville (Va.) Daily Progress*; Lang and Simmons.

SELECTED BIBLIOGRAPHY

REFERENCE WORKS

Chapman, Robert L. *American Slang*. New York: Harper Paperbacks, 1987.

Clay, Grady. *Real Places: An Unconventional Guide to America's Generic Landscape*. Chicago: University of Chicago Press, 1994.

Davidson, Mike, and Fay Dolnick, eds. *A Glossary of Zoning, Development, and Planning Terms*. Planning Advisory Service document 491–492. Chicago: American Planning Association, 1999.

Lighter, J. E. *Random House Historical Dictionary of American Slang*. New York: Random House, Vol. I, A-G, 1994; Vol. II, H-O, 1997.

Merriam-Webster's Collegiate Dictionary. Tenth edition. Springfield, MA: Merriam-Webster, 1993.

Moskowitz, Harvey S., and Carl G. Lindbloom. *The New Illustrated Book of Development Definitions*. New Brunswick, NJ: Center for Urban Policy Research, 1993. (Updated edition forthcoming in January 2004.)

Noll, Udo, and Peter Scupelli. *parole—a project of gruppo a12*. Online at http://parole.aporee.org.

Oxford English Dictionary. Online at http://dictionary.oed.com.

Reilly, John W. *The Language of Real Estate*. Chicago: Dearborn, 2000.

West, Bill W., and Richard L. Dickinson. *Street Talk in Real Estate*. Alameda, CA: Unique Publishing, 1987.

BOOKS AND ARTICLES CITED, WITH SOME FURTHER READING

Abramsky, Sasha. "Small-Town Blues: Building prisons is good business—just not for citizens." *American Prospect* 14 (June 2003): 19-21.

Alanen, Arnold, and Robert Melnick, eds. *Preserving Cul-*

tural Landscapes. Baltimore: Johns Hopkins University Press, 2000.

Arendt, Randall, et al. *Rural by Design.* Chicago: Planners Press, 1994.

Banerjee, Neela, and David Firestone. "New Kind of Electricity Market Strains Old Wires Beyond Limits." *The New York Times* (August 24, 2003): A1.

Beaumont, Constance E. *Better Models for Superstores: Alternatives to Big-Box Sprawl.* Washington, DC: National Trust for Historic Preservation, 1997.

———. *How Superstore Sprawl Can Harm Communities.* Washington, DC: National Trust for Historic Preservation, 1994.

Bierce, Ambrose. *The Devil's Dictionary.* 1911; reprint, New York: Dover, 1993.

Blake, Peter. *God's Own Junkyard: The Planned Deterioration of America's Landscape.* Rev. ed. New York: Holt, Rinehart, and Winston, 1979.

Blakely, Edward J., and Mary Gail Snyder. "Divided We Fall: Gated and Walled Communities in the United States." In *Architecture of Fear*, edited by Nan Ellin, 85-99. New York: Princeton Architectural Press, 1997.

Bullard, Robert D., Glenn S. Johnson, and Angel O. Torres. *Sprawl City: Race, Politics, and Planning in Atlanta.* Washington, DC: Island Press, 2000.

———, eds. *Highway Robbery: Transportation, Racism, and New Routes to Equity.* Cambridge: South End Press, forthcoming.

Burchell, Robert W., et al. *The Costs of Sprawl—Revisited.* Transportation Cooperative Research Program Report 39. Washington, DC: National Academy Press, 1998.

Butterfield, Fox. "Prison Rates Among Blacks Reach a Peak, Report Finds." *The New York Times* (April 7, 2003): A12.

Cagan, Joanna, and Neil deMause. *Field of Schemes: How the Great Stadium Swindle Turns Public Money into Private Profit.* Monroe, ME: Common Courage Press, 1999.

Calthorpe, Peter, and William Fulton. *The Regional City: Planning for the End of Sprawl.* Washington DC: Island Press, 2001.

Campanella, Thomas J. *Cities from the Sky: An Aerial Portrait of America.* New York: Princeton Architectural Press, 2001.

Campoli, Julie, Elizabeth Humstone, and Alex S. MacLean. *Above and Beyond: Visualizing Change in Small Towns and Rural Areas.* Chicago: American Planning Association, 2002.

Campoli, Julie, and Alex S. MacLean. "Visualizing Density." Working paper. Cambridge: Lincoln Institute for Land Policy, 2002.

Carbonell, Armando, and Lisa Cloutier. "Fifty Buzzwords: Key Words in Contemporary Land Policy in the United States." Presentation text. Cambridge: Lincoln Institute of Land Policy, November 2001.

Clay, Grady. *Strips: How to Read the American City.* Rev. ed. Chicago: University of Chicago Press, 1980.

Cohen, Lizabeth. *A Consumer's Republic: The Politics of Mass Consumption in Postwar America.* New York: Knopf, 2003.

Cohen, Stuart. "Sprawl Has Found Its Newest Enemy." *LightHawk* (Fall 2002): 1.

Daniels, Tom. *When City and Country Collide: Managing Growth in the Metropolitan Fringe.* Washington, DC: Island Press, 1999.

Downs, Anthony. "Some Realities about Sprawl and Urban Decline." *Housing Policy Debate* 10, 4 (1999): 955–974.

———. *Stuck in Traffic: Coping with Peak-Hour Traffic Congestion.* Washington, DC: Brookings Institution Press, 2003.

Duany, Andrés, Elizabeth Plater-Zyberk, and Jeff Speck. *Suburban Nation: The Rise of Sprawl and the Decline of the American Dream.* New York: North Point Press, 2000.

Duany Plater-Zyberk and Company. *The Lexicon of the New Urbanism.* Miami: DPZ, 1999.

Egan, Timothy. "Retail Darwinism Puts Old Malls in Jeopardy." *The New York Times* (January 1, 2000): A20.

Egerton, Brooks, and Reese Dunklin. "Government by Developer," *The Dallas Morning News* (June 10, 2001). Online at http://www.dallasnews.com/extra/0610 denton/index.html. (Accessed September 5, 2001.)

Feagin, Joe R., and Robert Parker. *Building American Cities: The Urban Real Estate Game.* 2nd ed. Englewood Cliffs, NJ: Prentice Hall, 1990.

Firey, Walter. "Ecological Considerations in Planning for Suburban Fringes." *American Sociological Review* 11 (1946): 411–23.

Fleming, Ronald Lee. *Saving Face: How Corporate Franchise Design Can Respect Community Identity.* Planning Advisory Service Report 452. Chicago: American Planning Association, 1994.

Floyd, Charles F., and Peter J. Shedd. *Highway Beautification: The Environmental Movement's Greatest Failure.* Boulder: Westview Press, 1979.

Fodor, Eben. *Better Not Bigger: How to Take Control of Urban Growth and Improve Your Community.* Gabriola Island, British Columbia: New Society Publishers, 1999.

Fogelson, Robert. *Downtown: Its Rise and Fall.* New Haven: Yale University Press, 2001.

Galster, George, Royce Hanson, Michael Ratcliffe, Hal Wolman, Stephen Coleman, and Jason Freihage. "Wrestling Sprawl to the Ground: Defining and Measuring an Elusive Concept." *Housing Policy Debate* 12 (2001): 681–717.

Garreau, Joel. *Edge City: Life on the New Frontier.* New York: Doubleday, 1991.

Gellner, Arrol. "California's Sound Wall Boondoggle." Inman News Features (2002). Online at http://doity-ourself.com/architecture/boondoggle.htm. (Accessed November 1, 2003.)

Gillham, Oliver. *The Limitless City: A Primer on the Urban Sprawl Debate.* Washington, DC: Island Press, 2002.

Goldsmith, William W. "Resisting the Reality of Race: Land Use, Social Justice, and the Metropolitan Economy." Cambridge: Lincoln Institute of Land Policy, 1999. Online at www.lincolninst.edu.

Gottdiener, Mark. *Planned Sprawl: Private and Public Interests in Suburbia.* Beverly Hills: Sage Publications, 1977.

Gratz, Roberta Brandes, and Norman Mintz. *Cities Back from the Edge.* New York: John Wiley, 1998.

Greenberg, Michael R., Frank J. Popper, and Bernadette M. West. "The TOADS: A New American Urban Epidemic." *Urban Affairs Quarterly* 25 (March 1990): 435–439.

Gudis, Catherine. *Buyways: Automobility, Billboards, and the American Cultural Landscape.* New York: Routledge, forthcoming.

Haberman, Clyde. "Of Huge Signs, Lamentations, and Re-zoning." *The New York Times* (December 20, 2000): B1.

Hayden, Dolores. *Building Suburbia: Green Fields and Urban Growth, 1820–2000.* New York: Pantheon, 2003.

———. *The Power of Place: Urban Landscapes as Public History.* Cambridge: MIT Press, 1995.

———. *Redesigning the American Dream: Gender, Housing, and Family Life.* Rev. ed. New York: W. W. Norton & Company, 2002.

———. "The Sense of Place and the Politics of Space." In *Understanding Ordinary Landscapes*, edited by Paul Groth and Todd Bressi. New Haven: Yale University Press, 1997: 111–133.

———, with photographs by Alex MacLean. "Aerial Photography on the Web: A New Tool for Community Debates on Land Use." *Lotus* 108 (Summer 2001), 118–131. (In Italian and English). Text without images also available online at www.lincolninst.edu.

Herbert, Bob. "Ball Pork." *The New York Times* (April 19, 1998): A17.

"How Does Your 'Burb Grow?" (editorial) Charlottes-ville, VA *Daily Progress*, (June 26, 2001): A8.

Huxtable, Ada Louise. *The Unreal America: Architecture and Illusion*. New York: New Press, 1997.

Jackson, John Brinckerhoff. *Landscape in Sight: Looking at America*. Edited by Helen Lefkowitz Horowitz. New Haven: Yale University Press, 1997.

———. "Truck City." In *The Car and the City: The Automobile, the Built Environment, and Daily Urban Life,* edited by Martin Wachs and Margaret Crawford, 16-24. Ann Arbor: University of Michigan Press, 1992.

Jacobs, Allan B. *Looking at Cities*. Cambridge: Harvard University Press, 1985.

Katz, Bruce, and Robert E. Lang, eds. *Redefining Urban and Suburban America: Evidence from Census 2000*. Washington, DC: Brookings Institution Press, 2003.

Kay, Jane Holtz. *Asphalt Nation: How the Automobile Took Over America and How We Can Get It Back*. New York: Crown, 1997.

Kilborn, Peter T. "The Flight Leaves Any Time, from the Backyard." *The New York Times* (April 17, 2002): A14.

———. "To Commute to Capital, Early Bird Gets 'Slugs.'" *The New York Times* (April 29, 2003): A22.

Knack, Ruth Eckdish. "Love Me, Love My Garage." *Planning* (June 2001). Online at www.planning.org/planning-practice/2001/june011.htm. (Accessed March 9, 2003.)

Kotkin, Joel. *The New Digital Geography: How the Digital Revolution Is Reshaping the American Landscape*. New York: Random House, 2000.

———, and Fred Siegel. *Digital Geography: The Remaking of City and Countryside in the New Economy*. Indianapolis: Hudson Institute, 2000.

Lang, Robert E. *Edgeless Cities: Exploring the Elusive Metropolis*. Washington, DC: Brookings Institution Press, 2003.

———. "Office Sprawl: The Evolving Geography of Business." Brookings Institution, Survey Series (October 2000). Online at www.brookings.edu/urban.

———, and Patrick A. Simmons. "Boomburbs: The Emergence of Large, Fast Growing Suburban Cities." In *Post-Suburbia: Examining the New Metropolitan Form*, 29–43 Washington DC: Fannie Mae Foundation, 2002.

Lerner, Steve. "Improve Your Lot: Robotic Parking Comes to New Jersey." *Amicus Journal* (Spring 2000): 19–20.

Levitt, B. Blake, ed. *Cell Towers: Wireless Convenience or Environmental Hazard?* Sheffield, MA: Berkshire-Litchfield Environmental Council, 2001.

Lewis, Peirce. " The Galactic Metropolis." In *Beyond the Urban Fringe*, edited by R. H. Platt and G. Macinko, 23-49. Minneapolis: University of Minnesota Press, 1983.

Lewis, Tom. *Divided Highways: Building the Interstate Highways, Transforming American Life*. New York: Penguin Putnam, 1997.

Liebs, Chester H. *Main Street to Miracle Mile: American Roadside Architecture*. Reprint. Baltimore: Johns Hopkins University Press, 1995.

Lipton, Eric. "City Trash Follows Long and Winding Road." *The New York Times* (March 24, 2001): B1-5.

Longstreth, Richard. *City Center to Regional Mall: Architecture, the Automobile, and Retailing in Los Angeles, 1920–1950*. Cambridge: MIT Press, 1997.

———. *The Drive-In, the Supermarket, and the Transformation of Commercial Space in Los Angeles, 1914–1941*. Cambridge: MIT Press, 2000.

McKenzie, Evan. *Privatopia: Homeowner Associations and the Rise of Residential Private Government*. New Haven: Yale University Press, 1994.

Marling, Karal Ann. *As Seen on TV: The Visual Culture of Everyday Life in the 1950s*. Cambridge: Harvard University Press, 1994.

Marx, Leo. "The American Ideology of Space." In *Denatured Visions: Landscape and Culture in the Twentieth Century*, edited by Stuart Wrede and W. H. Adams. New York: Museum of Modern Art, 1991.

Miller, Benjamin. *Fat of the Land: Garbage in New York the Last Two Hundred Years*. New York: Four Walls Eight Windows, 2000.

Miller, John. "Litter on a Stick: Billboards' Message: Go Ahead, Trash America." Online at http://www.scenic-florida.org.

Molotch, Harvey L. "The City as a Growth Machine: Toward a Political Economy of Place." *American Journal of Sociology* 82, 2 (1976): 309-332.

———, and John R. Logan. *Urban Fortunes: The Political Economy of Place*. Berkeley: University of California Press, 1987.

Nelessen, Anton. *Visions for a New American Dream*. Chicago: Planners Press, 1994.

Newhall, Beaumont. *Airborne Camera: The World from the Air and Outer Space*. New York: Hastings House, 1969.

Orfield, Myron. *American Metropolitics: The New Suburban Reality*. Washington, DC: Brookings Institution Press, 2002.

Peirce, Neal R. "Big-Box Dinosaurs and the Urban Tar Pits." *Baltimore Sun* (December 4, 1995).

Pile, Steve, and Nigel Thrift, eds. *City a/z*. New York: Routledge, 2000.

Real Estate Research Corporation. *The Costs of Sprawl: Environmental and Economic Costs of Alternative Residential Developments Patterns at the Urban Fringe*. Washington, DC: United States Government Printing Office, 1974.

Register, Richard. "Depaving the World." *Culture Change*. On line at http://www.culture change.org/issue 10/rregister.html (Accessed March 8, 2003)

Rome, Adam. *The Bulldozer in the Countryside: Suburban Sprawl and the Rise of American Environmentalism*. New York: Cambridge University Press, 2001.

Rose, Mark H. *Interstate: Express Highway Politics, 1939–1989*. Rev. ed. Knoxville: University of Tennessee Press, 1990.

Sandweiss, Martha A. "Introduction," vii–xiii. In *William Garnett: Aerial Photographer*. Berkeley: University of California Press, 1994.

Schlosser, Eric. *Fast Food Nation: The Dark Side of the American Meal*. New York: Houghton Mifflin, 2001.

Selingo, Jeffrey. "Talking More but Enjoying It Less." *The New York Times* (February 14, 2002): G1.

Squires, Gregory D., ed. *Urban Sprawl: Causes, Consequences, and Policy Responses*. Washington, DC: The Urban Institute Press, 2002.

Squires, Michael. "U.S. 95 Stretch to Get Sound Wall." *Las Vegas Review-Journal* (September 18, 2003). Online at http://www.reviewjournal.com.

Szold, Terry, and Armando Carbonell, eds. *Smart Growth: Form and Consequences*. Cambridge: Lincoln Institute of Land Policy, 2002.

"Two Million Inmates, and Counting" (editorial). *The New York Times* (April 9, 2003): A18.

Valentine, Maggie. *The Show Starts on the Sidewalk*. New Haven: Yale University Press, 1993.

Venturi, Robert, Denise Scott Brown, and Steven Izenour. *Learning from Las Vegas: The Forgotten Symbolism of Architectural Form*. Rev. ed. Cambridge: MIT Press, 1977.

Weiss, Michael J. *The Clustered World: How We Live, What We Buy, and What It All Means About Who We Are*. Boston: Little, Brown, 2000.

Weitz, Jerry. *Sprawl Busting: State Programs to Guide Growth*. Chicago: Planners Press, 1999.

Wikle, Thomas A., "Cellular Tower Proliferation in the United States." *Geographical Review*, 92, 1 (January 2002): 45–62.

Woodside, Christine. "Cell Towers Are Sprouting in Unlikely Places." *The New York Times* (January 9, 2000): CT1.

WEBSITES

Architecture, Planning, Environment

American Farmland Trust http://www.farmland.org
American Planning Association http://www.planning.org
Center for Land Use Interpretation http://www.clui.org
Coalition Against Public Funding for Stadiums
    http://www.stopballpork.org
Congress for the New Urbanism http://www.cnu.org
LightHawk http://www.lighthawk.org
Lincoln Institute of Land Policy
    http://www.lincolninst.edu
National Building Museum http://www.nbm.org
National Trust for Historic Preservation
    http://www.nationaltrust.org
Natural Resources Defense Council
    http://www.nrdc.org
Planners Network Online
    http://www.plannersnetwork.org
Scenic America http://www.scenic.org
Sierra Club http://www.sierraclub.org
Smart Growth America http://www.smartgrowthameri-ca.com
Urban Land Institute http://www.uli.org
Vermont Forum on Sprawl http://www.vtsprawl.org

Government

Central Region Energy Resources Team
    http://energy.cr.usgs.gov/energy/stats_ctry
Department of Sanitation, New York City
    http://www.ci.nyc.ny.us
Energy Information Administration
    http://www.eia.doe.gov
Environmental Protection Agency http://www.epa.org
Federal Highway Administration
    http://www.fhwa.dot.gov
United States Census http://www.census.gov
United States Department of Housing and Urban Development (inclues FHA) http://www.hud.gov/offices.hsg

Corporations and Trade Associations

American Automobile Manufacturers Association
    http://www.aama.com
Cellular Telecommunications and Internet Association
    http://www.wow-com.com
International Council of Shopping Centers
    http://www.icsc.com
McDonald's http://www.mcdonalds.com
National Asphalt Pavement Association
    http://www.hotmix.org
National Association of Home Builders
    http://www.nahb.org
National Association of Realtors http://www.realtor.org
North American Truck Stop Network
    http://www.natsn.com
Outdoor Advertising Organization of America
    http://www.oaaa.org
Wal-Mart Stores, Inc. http://www.walmart.com

INDEX

Main entries are in **bold**.